I KNOW WHAT TO DO! SOCIAL SKILLS

HOW TO LISTEN

CAITIE MCANENEY

PowerKiDS press

Published in 2025 by The Rosen Publishing Group, Inc.
2544 Clinton Street, Buffalo, NY 14224

First Edition

Editor: Caitie McAneney
Book Design: Rachel Rising

Photo Credits: Cover, p.1 Pressmaster/Shutterstock.com; pp. 2, 4, 6, 8, 10, 12, 14, 15, 16, 18, 20 Cute art/Shutterstock.com; pp. 5, 17 Monkey Business Images/Shutterstock.com; p. 7 Asti Mak/Shutterstock.com; p. 9 wavebreakmedia/Shutterstock.com; p. 11 shisu_ka/Shutterstock.com; p. 13 Drazen Zigic/Shutterstock.com; p. 15 PeopleImages.com - Yuri A/Shutterstock.com; p. 19 pics five/Shutterstock.com; p. 21 SeventyFour/Shutterstock.com.

Library of Congress Cataloging-in-Publication Data

Names: McAneney, Caitie, author.
Title: How to listen / Caitie McAneney.
Description: Buffalo, NY : PowerKids Press, [2025] | Series: I know what to do! social skills | Includes index.
Identifiers: LCCN 2024031207 (print) | LCCN 2024031208 (ebook) | ISBN 9781499450545 (library binding) | ISBN 9781499450538 (paperback) | ISBN 9781499450552 (ebook)
Subjects: LCSH: Listening–Juvenile literature. | Social skills–Study and teaching–Juvenile literature.
Classification: LCC BF323.L5 M362 2025 (print) | LCC BF323.L5 (ebook) | DDC 153.6/8–dc23/eng/20240710
LC record available at https://lccn.loc.gov/2024031207
LC ebook record available at https://lccn.loc.gov/2024031208

Manufactured in the United States of America

CPSIA Compliance Information: Batch #CWPK25. For Further Information contact Rosen Publishing at 1-800-237-9932.

CONTENTS

Listen Up 4
Zip It! 6
Active Listening. 8
Understanding 10
Make New Friends. 12
Talk It Out 14
Learn Something New. 16
Follow Directions. 18
A Good Listener 20
Glossary 22
For More Infomation 23
Index .24

Listen Up

You probably hear things every day. But do you know how to listen? Listening is an important skill. You can listen to your parents, teachers, and friends. When you listen to someone, you can learn something new. You can connect with the person.

Zip It!

How can you be a good listener? Zip your lips. Be quiet. Let the other person talk. You can talk when they're done. If you talk over someone, you won't really hear what they have to say.

Active Listening

Active listening is when you give your full **attention** to someone. It takes practice. Stop what you are doing. Turn to the person. Make **eye contact**. Listen to their words. What are they saying? What do they mean?

Understanding

Take a moment to think. What did the person say? Maybe they told you how they feel. Maybe they asked you to do something. Try not to **judge** the person. Try to understand how they feel and what they want. Then, you can **respond**.

Make New Friends

How can you use listening skills? You can use them when you meet people. You can get to know the person. Ask them questions. Then, listen to their answers. Now, you can share with them. You may make a new friend!

Talk It Out

Sometimes people are upset. They need to talk it out. You can talk to someone when you are upset. You can also listen to someone else. Ask them what's wrong. Listen to them with your full attention. You don't have to say anything.

PRACTICE MAKES PROGRESS!

When someone seems upset, you can say:

"You look upset. Do you want to talk about it?"

"I am here to listen."

"What happened?"

"I have big feelings too sometimes. It helps me to talk about it."

Learn Something New

You can learn a lot from listening. Your parent may teach you how to wash dishes or make a bed. Your friend may teach you how to score a goal. Your teacher may teach you how to read. If you don't listen, you can't learn.

Follow Directions

Following directions is important in school and at home. Your parents may tell you how to get ready for school. If you listen carefully, you can do each step. Then, you can leave for school on time. Following directions helps you work together.

A Good Listener

Good listeners **focus** on the people they're with. They make good friends. They learn new things. They help people who need to talk about their feelings. If you listen to others, they will listen to you. Being a good listener is important!

GLOSSARY

attention: The act of directing your mind to something, especially by listening or watching.

eye contact: The act of two people looking at each other's eyes.

focus: To direct your attention to something.

judge: To decide if something or someone is right or wrong.

respond: To answer or reply to something.

FOR MORE INFORMATION

BOOKS

Adams, Kenneth. *Listening to Others*. New York, NY: Rosen Publishing Group, 2021.

Rose, Emily. *Making and Keeping Friends*. Ann Arbor, MI: Cherry Lake Publishing, 2022.

WEBSITES

Life's Little Lessons: Friendship
pbskids.org/learn/lifes-little-lessons/friendship/
Explore ways to be a good friend and listener with Daniel Tiger and PBS Kids.

Talking About Your Feelings
kidshealth.org/en/kids/talk-feelings.html
Learning how to talk about your feelings can help you listen to others. Check out this page for great tips.

INDEX

A
attention, 8, 14

E
eye contact, 8

F
feelings, 10, 15, 20
focus, 20
following directions, 18
friends, 4, 12, 16, 20

G
good listeners, 6, 20

H
helping, 20
home, 18

L
learning, 4, 16, 20
listening skills, 4, 12

P
parent, 4, 16, 18

T
teacher, 4, 16